D0532496

CASUAL SEX
and other verse

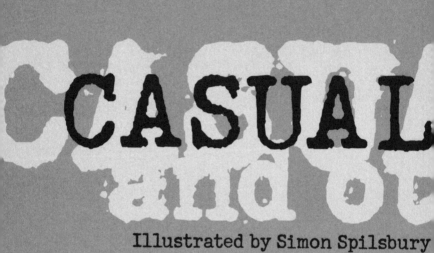

Illustrated by Simon Spilsbury

Murray Lachlan Young

SEX

and other verse

BANTAM BOOKS

TORONTO · NEW YORK · LONDON · SYDNEY · AUCKLAND

CASUAL SEX AND OTHER VERSE
A BANTAM BOOK : 0 553 50693 5

First publication in Great Britain.

PRINTING HISTORY
Bantam edition published 1997

Bantam Books are published by Transworld Publishers Ltd,
61-63 Uxbridge Road, London W5 5SA,
in Australia by Transworld Publishers (Australia) Pty Ltd,
15-25 Helles Avenue, Moorebank, NSW 2170,
and in New Zealand by Transworld Publishers (NZ) Ltd,
3 William Pickering Drive, Albany, Auckland.

Reproduced, printed and bound in Great Britain by
Mackays of Chatham PLC, Chatham, Kent

Acknowledgements

Special thanks in no particular order to

Zoë

Hamish

Alistair Young Snr

Penelope Young

Adam Unsworth

Trever Adams

James Burfitt

Steve Buckwald

Jane Collier

Long

J J

Stanley

Pete & Bob

Tom Mortimer

Michael Howlett

Debbie D

Stuart Lyon

Jean Findley

Spencer

Kevin Pertillo

Morcheeba

Rebecca CWV

Chris Warmsley

Shadowe + Tru Love

Dameon

The Artists formerly

known as Shriekback

Paul MacDonald

Dr R Posner

Pandora Mellie

Roland Metcalf

Colin Muir

Steve Dixon

Robbie Jones

George MacDonald

Frazer

Jenny Wittaker

All at Transworld

Lisa & Georgina

Sally Homer

Raz Gold

Steve Kutner

Grant Black

Old Black Ged

Apologies

to anyone I missed

Extra special

thanks to

David Beaumont

Contents

CASUAL SEX
and other verse

Casual Sex

They met in a bar close to San Moritz
They reconvened at a suite in the Ritz
They ordered hors d'oeuvres and drank several gin slings
Then ruthlessly chatted of meaningless things.

Him dressed in lightweight safari suit
Her dressed in lounge wear of cool pastel silk
Made a rendezvous on a deep-pile carpet
Exchanging neat gambits of Catholic guilt
Not a mark on their skin
Not a hair out of place
A remarkable feat of high aquiline grace – they had

Cazual sex

Him in pith helmet and her in high heels

Cazual sex

He gave a volley of well-rehearsed groans
Whilst she was restricted to hamster-like squeals

Cazual sex

Oh their fine-smelling feet did not once leave the ground
For they both reappeared in Burmese dressing gowns
    after,

        cazual sex

There in a haze of eau de toilette
She casually lit two international-length cigarettes
And said:

> '*Luxury goods, luxury goods,*
> *I've had my eye on luxury goods.*
> *Luxury goods, luxury goods,*
> *I've had my eye on luxury goods.*

'Armani, *Versace*, *Versace*, Armani,
Versace, Armani, Armani oh *yes!*

'Cartier, Dunhill, perpetual self-winding
                                    Rolex Oyster,
Christian Dior, Chanel, Ralph Lauren, Lancôme,
Givenchy, Boss Boss Hugo, Mont Blanc, Pierre
Cardin, ooh ooh Jimmy Choo,
Issey Miyake, Prada, Prada, Prada, Hermes,
L'Egoiste, L'Egoiste,
Ferrero Rocher,

Oh, Oh, Oh, Oh duty free!'

The Boy Who Put His Love On Sale

He pushed up the flap that led to the attic
the decision had been taken it was quite automatic.
The note had been signed,
the noose had been tied.
He kicked away the chair with style and aplomb,
but instead of feeling his spinal cord snap
his feet hit the ground with a tiresome slap.
The stupid boy had got it wrong –
he'd gone and tied the rope too long!

Picture if you will a girl on a plane
now picture a boy who believes he's to blame.
The girl to Japan
and the boy to his room,
a waster, quite useless,
a song without tune.

Now when we lose our self-esteem
there comes an old unwritten law,
that strange persuasive salesmen do come knocking at our door
and McLeash was so slow in his bitter reflection,

Who Put On Sale

he warranted quite an unusual attention.
For noon of that day a specialist had quietly come to town
young children on their way home from school had said
they'd heard a laughing sound.

That came from near the bus stop
or someone said the sweet shop
and others said they'd smelt a smell
that left them feeling light of head.
And when their mothers heard this
they sent their children straight to bed.
For they all knew the time had come
to pull the blind and bolt the door,
because the fair had come again
to entertain upon the moor.
But McLeash sat alone
with his eye on the phone
or expecting a letter to come *par avion*.
So it was no great surprise
when the note hit the doormat
and the long-legged man in the small bowler hat

did stealthily stride from McLeash's garden path
with a sound that I swear was a dry hollow laugh.
As his high-stepping stride danced him over the wall
diving into the darkness, a trace, oh so small,
drifted back on the night spawning fast on the breeze
and that smell I declare with the greatest of ease
was the scent to which all our young hearts were once lost
yes, the sickly sweet smell of fairground candyfloss,
softly stole through the keyhole and under the door,
through the cracks in the window and up through the floor
wrapping helpless McLeash in its soft crimson cloak,
then the note on the mat through the mist gently spoke
in a sugary chant no young man could resist,
first seduced by the metre and then gently kissed.
As the rhyme's fingers ran through his hair
the decision was taken to go to the fair.

So let's miss out the journey
pretend that we're there
and we'll focus our thoughts
on the free thinkers' fair.
And off McLeash did quietly go
'Tween all the brightly coloured sideshows
of men with three legs, dogs with two heads
and monkeys duelling on a razor's edge
with buzzing chainsaws
and then McLeash saw
a sign bright and bold
which read 'EMOTIONS BOUGHT & SOLD'.

Transfixed, the boy approached the tent
                    and slowly looked inside
and through the scented misty air he spied a pair of eyes
and then he heard a voice to match the brightly glowing orbs
hypnotic forces pulling him away
                    from all the ordinary folk outside.
McLeash's mind did start to slip and start to slide
into the bony outstretched hand of he they called

'The Peddler Man'

who sat legs akimbo on a piebald rocking horse.
    'Ah McLeash!' the peddler said,

'Come in. I've waited and, of course,
you've never seen a donkey win the Derby,'
said the man
'or met a chap on roller skates
who balanced twenty flans upon his nose.
Would you suppose
that possibly this could be true?
I ask as a fellow lover of the Highland stew
that you had in Dumfries
when you were thirteen at least
or was it thirteen and two thirds,
and oh how you laughed my pretty young thing
when your father showed you those talking birds
that repeated your phrases with perfect precision
and then yes, of course, that dreadful collision
with the man who rode the motorbike
your father thought your mother liked.
Oh tell me, McLeash, was his death neatly planned
and just what would you do for to go to Japan?'

conspiratorially winking his eye.
The peddler gestured as if he could fly

flapping his arms like the wings of a bird
looking really quite absurd
between you and me.

But McLeash could not see
hooded, obliviously blissfully blinkered.
McLeash was reeled in –
hook, line and sinker.

So it came to pass that McLeash in hot blood
signed his full name in triplicate, trading his love
for a choice of beef or salmon
on the night flight out of town.

So let's jump ahead to Tokyo
and watch his plane touch down
but the runway is bare, the plane is not there
for a terrorist's bomb did explode in midair.

The Life
of

The Life & Death of Art

Half man half prawn reclining on a corned-beef chaise longue
Yes, contemporary art is what I speak of
And half man half prawn was its searing blade
Until one balmy night near the end of high summer
A new ace was pulled from the tumbling deck
A trump card produced and then cunningly played.

The gallery was rammed and buzzing
In high expectation of what was to come
Some said an act of pure existentialism
Others a mixture of Dada and Jung
There had been some confusion just by the main door
For a Shih Tzu had laid a small turd on the floor
Hence a group from the art school
Had left their depression
Declaring a spontaneous act of expression
In short it was just too avant-garde
The rumours were running like molten lard.

Did the sperm come from Dali
The egg from Fonteyn

Art & Death

The artist-cum-surgeon
A fast-breaking name
The surrogate mother knew what was expected
For her broken waters had been shaken and stirred
By the funky bartender so cool and connected
Frankincense burned as the dour dilettante
Sipped on his cool embryonic frappé
The heavily pregnant birth mother entered
And a bearded philanthropist shouted '*Olé*!'
Murmurs rose as she stepped on the canvas
Clad in polyandrous birthing smock
A guru's low mantra rang out from the Tannoy
(Nam myoho renge kyo)
The lights were dimmed low until but one single spot
Illuminated the birth of the innocent child.

Tiny silent bright on bare white canvas
An act of creation quite second to none
Tiny silent bright on bare white canvas
Unaware of its role in a cruel world to come.

Tarquin Mule the artist-cum-surgeon
Stepped forward and snipped the umbilical cord
Then adjusting his black raw-silk surgeon's gown
Held the child aloft as though addressing the Lord

> *'I proclaim this child to be all that is art*
> *And all that is art to be this child*
> *Its name will be Art*
> *And so will its nature*
> *So let's kick off the bidding*
> *In honour of Nietzsche.'*

Pepe Le Blanc the celebrity chef
Bore the afterbirth off on a cold silver tray
The birth mother sedated was put in a car
As he feverishly started to flip and flambé
And by the time he had served up his radically chic canapé
The bloodstained canvas and baby boy
Had been snapped up and wrapped up and driven away.

> Art's life was brief and uninspiring
> Because everything Art touched turned to *art*
> Fifty soiled nappies behind tinted Perspex
> His first work sold for the price of a theme park
> Schooled in a gallery cut from glass
> A contemporary mariner tied to the mast
> Of his life on a windless sea
> Poor Art became lonely as lonely can be.

By the age of twenty he'd grossed twelve billion
But at last found love with a girl named Vermillion
Who ran her own public relations firm
The promotion of art was its sole concern.

She told him he was a living god
And fed him with pink analgesic pills
She told him whatever he wanted to hear
(She was in PR for Christ's sake, it was her job)
And Art paid the bills.

But oh what a day
What a catastrophic shock
When Art returned home from his self-help group
To find his bedroom door firmly locked
The Bentley estate parked behind the wall
The half-empty bottle of vintage Krug
The surgeon's gown on the floor in the hall
He peeked through the keyhole
His heart in his throat
To see Vermillion *in flagrante delicto*
Tied hand and foot
With a raw-silk rope.

The correspondent it was plain to see
Was Tarquin Mule, his mentor, creator

Yes, Tarquin Mule, that villainous fiend.

On a dark and dusty old factory floor
Art first shed his clothes before bolting the door

He mounted the gibbet of improvised crates
Contemplating his life in its tragical fate
He tied up the noose, said a short prayer
Broken-hearted, spent and ruined
He closed his dull eyes
Then kicked the cold air.

But the instant he did
Twenty floodlights flashed on
And surrounded he was by a chattering throng
Of champagne-sipping bourgeoisie
Art critics, socialites, national TV and radio crews
All there to peruse
But most disgustingly
Most disgracefully
Most outrageously
Tarquin Mule
Powdered and cruel
Hemp-clad and nimble
Jumped up on a stool.

'*Witness my friends,*
the death of Art'
(Tarquin spoke working
the room like a tart)
With a snap of his fingers
A black canvas was laid
Beneath poor twitching Art
For his swansong to play.

It is said the last motion of a hanging man
Is ejaculation
And there according to Tarquin's heinous plan
The last drops of life
Spilt forth from Art's trembling form
Hit the canvas stark and bare
There in death
His last work was born.

The exhibition lasted ninety days
Whilst Art turned green and rotted away
Tarquin and Vermillion moved to LA
And still live there now I've heard people say.

So the moral is clear and the moral is plain
In this case I'm afraid only *art* is to blame
So believe what you wish
Or believe who you are
But please make sure above all else
That you never ever ever believe in your own PR.

Action &
Consequence

Action & Consequence

Bungee

jumping

can

be

fun

but

poor

Alfredo

weighed

a ton.

Simply Everyone's Taking Cocaine

From Mayfair to Morden,
from Soho to Sidcup,
from Richmond to Dalston,
through old Regent's Park.

From Borough to Bayswater,
Crouch End to Clapham,
from Debden to Tooting,
beneath Marble Arch.

There are daughters of ministers,
children of clergy,
There are amiable Honourables – barristers
verging on every single section
of today's society
have thrown figs to the wind
and embraced with such glee
the most wonderful pastime
to have come around in years.
Yes, policemen and plumbers,
roadsweepers and peers.

everyone's Cocaine

Simply everyone's taking cocaine.

At sports day in villages, cities and towns
world records are breaking, they just can't slow down.
In the fathers' race one chap whilst rushing at speed
had recorded a time just below 8.03
and that was the four hundred metres.
He had holidayed near Costa Rica.

Simply everyone's taking cocaine.

Well I saw Fizzy Sipworth last Saturday night,
and her eyes seemed to blaze with a wonderful light.
I said, 'Fizzy, my darling, you look quite divine.'
She said, 'You would do too, if you'd just had a line.'

Simply everyone's taking cocaine.

Well I saw a young officer pounding his beat.
I said, 'Officer why are you grinding your teeth?'
He said, 'You should try walking ten miles sir,
and now I can jump twenty stiles sir.'

Simply everyone's taking cocaine – sir!

Well I saw Aunt Milly in last season's clothes,
she said car, house and yacht
had gone straight up her nose.
But she'd had a most wonderful time,
and the whole thing seemed simply sublime.
I said, 'Milly, my dear, you'll be dead at this rate.'
'Not at all,' parried she, 'for I've just had a plate
made of metal put into my nose.'
Now she's hoovering it up like a hose.

Simply everyone's taking cocaine.

Well I saw Uncle Berty, he danced on the table.
I said, 'Berty you're past it and surely not able.'
'Precisely my boy, I am past eighty-three,
and you would dance just the same
if you'd hoofed a whole 'G'*
of Colombian straight from the rock.'
Berty's death was no terrible shock.
So off to the funeral, off to the wake,
we were all in an underexuberant state
till the point where things were so dead at twenty past nine
Aunty Milly said cheekily, 'Let's have a line,'
and we all shouted hip hip hurrah!

Simply everyone's taking cocaine.

For bus drivers are tooting it,
jockeys are hoofing it,

*Gram. User's terminology.

31

DJs are spinning it,
gamblers are winning it,
forces manoeuvring it,
cleaners are hoovering it,
models are booked on it,
anglers are hooked on it,
pensioners drawing it,
footballers scoring it,
technicians miking it,
PAs are biking it,
producers are trying it,
A&R men denying it.
publishers collecting it,
lawyers protecting it,
artists are begging it,
some of them pegging it.
It seems that it's simple,
there's no-one to blame,
for the whole of this nation
is taking cocaine.

Simply everyone's taking cocaine.

Oh how gay it all seems,
and how bright we all are.
How much fun we are having,
and oh what a lark,
to have blistering jousting and sharp repartee
Oh please less less less about you

And please more more more about me!

The Super Model

The Super Model
            had a *super* night
At the *super* restaurant
            it was such a *super* sight
When she *super* danced
            at the *super* nightclub
With the *super* people
            wearing *super* clothes
To the *super* tunes
            of the *super* DJ
And then for the world's press
            she *super* posed
But when they asked her
            how her life had been
She just smiled and said,
'It's been really wicked!'

The Boy Who Struck the Recording Deal
(W.A.H. Wiggins)

The boy who struck the recording deal
was a boy with a nervous unlikely appeal.
He had platinum teeth,
he had solid gold hair,
his young eyes were like mirrors
his soul was quite bare.
So it was odd
when he was found drowned
unrecouped in the swimming pool.

The muffled tone of a mobile phone
rang twice from the depths of a silken-lined suit.
A fast black Mercedes sped onto the scene,
a bag with a zip tumbled into the boot.
A plane touched down on a private airstrip,
a stretcher appeared and the bag was removed.
A young star disappeared
                    and the press mourned his death,

Struck the Deal

whilst great rumours were spread
        and small clues were removed.
Whilst they froze the boy with the recording deal
and they froze his quite nervous unlikely appeal,
and they froze his gold hair
        and his bright shining teeth,
and they sunk him in nitrogen and my belief
is he joined all the others who died for the cause
in a cryogenic talent bank somewhere abroad
still under contract frozen in time.

        Golden Children of the Revolution...

The Pros & Cons of Superstardom

Where is my leopardskin stretch limousine?
Where is the stuff of my star-studded dream?
Where is my villa in the south of France?
Where are all those sexy girls who meet me just by chance?
Where is the Arab steed I ride across the beach?
Where are the keys to my Bentley Corniche?
Where are the parties by the giant-sized pool?
Where are all my newfound friends who
tell me I'm just so cool?

Where are the charities knocking at the door?
Where are the Dobermanns to keep away the poor?
Where is my castle in Beverly Hills?
Where is my drawer full of purple sleeping pills?
Where is my bitter and twisted biographer?
Where are the bushes containing photographers?
Where is the stalker who lurks in the park?
Where is my fear of being left in the dark?

Where's my gerbil?
Where's my hamster?
Where's my guru?
Where's my mantra?
Where's my neurosis?
Where's my psychosis?
Where is my strange and dysfunctional child?

I'm Being Followed
By the Rolling Stones

I have something to tell you.
I'm being followed by the Rolling Stones.

> They followed me here and they'll follow me home.
> They turn up at nightclubs and parties and bars
> trying to make me drink beer and talk about art.
> They camp in my garden
> they won't let me rest they ring my phone
> they're completely obsessed.

I'm being followed by the Rolling Stones.

> And that skinny one, thingamy, you know his name,
> the one with the big lips, well he's mainly to blame,
> for he comes round in girls' clothes when I'm all alone
> then looks through his fringe and says,

'Oi, is Charlie at home?'*

* To be said in a Jaggeresque tone.

I'm being followed by the Rolling Stones.

I can't go anywhere unmolested.
I can't fight back they'd have me arrested.
I feel like a lunatic no-one believes me.
It doesn't make sense and lest no-one can see
the shadow they cast on my innocent life.
Oh they think it's so funny and so do their wives.

And that Texan, *oh yes*, she's the head of the bunch,
making personal comments while I'm eating lunch.
Criticizing just because I don't know
                        how to order in French
Couchez avec moi ce soir
I don't know what that is
Or what it tastes like.
They think it's a laugh and they think it's a joke,
but they're driving me close to the end of a rope!

I'm being followed by the Rolling Stones.

The Tale of Clifton Smelchard
(The Butcher's Son)

> Children playing in the fields
> Laughing skipping making cartwheels
> Fishing paddling in the brook
> Mother's dress pin makes their angling hooks
> Oh happy times when the sun shone all day
> But what of those who went astray?

This is the story of meat my friends
So any vegetarians
Who find offal quite awful
And ham not so glamorous
That tales of prime beef make you feel quite forlorn
I suggest that you leave in your leatherette shoes
and return to your homes and eat – tofu.

> Clifton Smelchard the butcher's lad
> A healthy boy but quite a young tearaway
> Yes Clifton with his chunky thighs
> Would kiss the girls and make them cry

Smelchard

And sometimes even kiss the boys
To which his father shouted, '*Oi!*
Stop that lark, you cheeky lad
You know what happens when you're bad.'*
And everybody knew too well
The butcher put his lad through hell
For however fast young Cliff could run
He could not escape a whole ox tongue
Brought down with force by P. J. Smelchard
With the lustful cry of
'*Think that was hard – did you my little man?*
Well, my father beat me with a whole cured ham
And remember naughty cousin Leicester
Caught with three mince-filled French letters
Smuggling them out to the local co-op
Selling them so he could go off

* To be spoken in a Leicestershire accent.

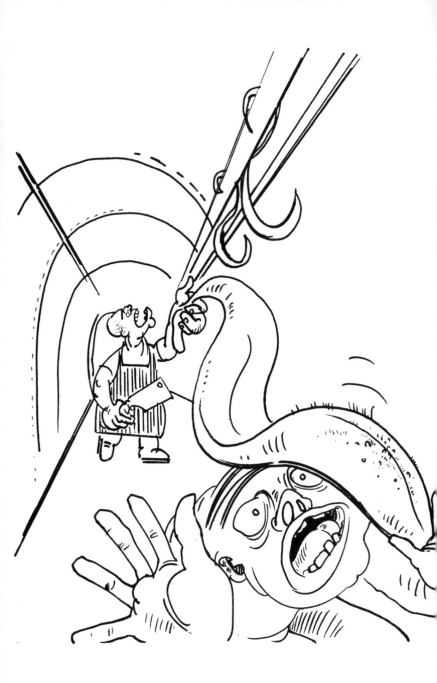

In his mother's motor car to drink champagne and la-di-da
With three young toffs from the local college
Claiming he was gaining knowledge
Of some technique or new appliance
Of uphill agricultural science
No wonder poor old Uncle Arthur
Strung him from the kitchen rafter
With a string of chipolata sausages
And all the local villagers
Dined high on Smelchard's
Minced pork pies
But no-one ever did enquire
Just why those luscious juicy pies
Did somehow come
     from Leicestershire.

'So my clever little mister,'
In falsetto P. J. whispered,
'Just watch where you put those plates
For trade has not been good of late.'

Thus my friends it may be trusted
That young Cliff came maladjusted
                    Bloodstained from this dynasty
                    Of offal tripe and fatty horsemeat
And continuous floggings with poor cuts of beef
Makes me feel quite content in my long-held belief
That 'twas fate that stepped in on a night late in May
When young Clifton was met near the abattoir playing
By sight of a hobbling hulk of a youth
                    Yes quite blackened of eye
                    And quite bloodshot of tooth
                    His name was Rowan Jeroboam
                    And he was the vintner's son
And Rowan Jeroboam had of late a red-faced boy become
For though he stood both wide and stout
Young Jeroboam suffered gout
A state which was quite solely brought
                    about by a love of vintage port
And Rowan guzzled night and day
But at just ten years could not pay
For this hobby by means which most young lads find
                    Like paper rounds or mowing kind
                    Old ladies' grassy lawns.
No this oddball was amorally drawn
To a different type of child labour
Self-employed young Rowan favoured
Burning rubber pumping bass
            Wailing sirens high-speed chases
                    Thrills and spills and spinning wheels

Yes smashing windows robbing tills.
In simple terms this young invader
Would be termed today in tabloid press
As nothing less than a
Ravaging
    Raptorial
        Ransacking
            Ram Raider

And it didn't take long for young Cliff to belong
To this quite exclusive gentleman's club
No it didn't take long for young Cliff to go along
Wearing false ginger beard to the local nightclub
With Rowan flashing his five-pound notes
And plying poor Clifton with Malibu and Coke
And it wasn't very long before off the boys sped
With sixteen valves screaming rev counter on red
Blasting fast past the CID who were busily observing
The public toilets through a hole in the roof
For the ninth week running
               because they needed more proof
And up to ninety miles an hour
               with prepubescent shrieks they powered
Clifton oblivious the final stop
               would be his father's butcher's shop

Where at that very moment behind blood-red
Blind stood P. J. chewing on soft bacon rind
The chairman of one, dare I mention,
          clandestine local butchers' convention
Where six dark figures stood in rapt delight

Displaying prime beef beneath candlelight
With choppers twitching in their hands these butchers
Were cunningly hatching a plan.

'We'll have six dozen pies from him,'

           said old Uncle Arthur.

               'With the rest we'll have sausages.'

And there amid incestuous laughter
The butchers danced their terrible dance
To work themselves into a murderous trance
Which would end in young Cliff being dragged
From his bed for the butchers to delight
                in his hideous bloodshed
     But they didn't know what we know
     Or that Clifton's empty bed
          was stuffed with three goosefeather pillows
     Or for that matter their own dreadful part
     In this sanguine truly disparate farce
     So now hold tight onto your seat
     While I reveal the *coup de grâce*

Wam bam battering ram
        through the plate glass Rowan slammed

The bull bar on his car's front end
Bringing lives of four butchers to a timely end
And Rowan gave his own last wheezing gasp
Impaled on a shimmering shard of glass.

Old Arthur gave such a bloodthirsty cheer,

'We've got enough meat here to last us a year.'

And then he turned his nihilist's glare
On Clifton

'You my lad, yes *you* my lad
Will do medium rare.'

Then he turned to P. J. who was far from dead
With a great cleaver aloft shouting,

'Off with his head'

So together they readied to deliver the final death blow
Their blades became stayed with the shrill cry of

'Noo Noo Noo!'

They turned to the place from whence the voice had come
To their shock horror and amazement

It was the ghost of Arthur's only begotten son
P. J.'s nephew Clifton's cousin
You remember Leicester
The boy who was sold for a tenner a dozen?
Pies
mince pork pies
And all his tortured hollow cries
Put fear in their hearts,
turned their thick legs to jelly
Arthur lost control of his bowels

and sadly committed harikari.

Return your mind to the gruesome picture
Of a vintner's son and five dead butchers
　　　Clifton and P. J. standing face to face
Father and son creator and created both products
　　　　　of our human race.

　　　　　Now I won't insult your intelligence
　　　　　By explaining in detail the rest of the plot
　　　　　Or of the further heinous crimes
　　　　　Committed by P. J. the provincial despot
　　　　　Or of what befell poor Clifton
　　　　　Because I would say that it spoke for itself
　　　　　And after all my main concern lies purely in the
　　　　　Interest of public health

So I shall just give you a warning – a little advice
Be certain never at any price
To go near a place known as Groapingham Common
And buy their pork pies which are flavoured with port
Even if a drive thru' butcher's
　　　　　seems such a wonderfully novel thought
If the slogan

'Meat for Life'

　　　　　shines from the window like a tempting pun
Be certain never ever to go near one of six
　　　　　fine butcher's shop
owned by Clifton Smelchard & Son.

Comeback Tour

A stadium filled with middle-aged males
Squeezed into tight pants with bald heads and ponytails
Beer guts and beefburgers
Lawyers and roadworkers
Not a woman seen within the nearest twenty miles
Brooding testosterone
bonding with high-fives thrown
all waiting for the clomp of the platform heel
For the sight of the Lycra-clad barrel-waisted rock star
heavy metal thunder
A plank-spanking solo squeal.

I'm fairly sure it was a comeback tour.

Just Anot
th

Just Another Night at the Seaside

It was just another night at the seaside.
The tide had come in and the sun had gone down
the shutters were up, the blank day had been drowned.
There was flickering light from the pier's sad remains
a charred and smoking skeletal monument
                        hissing salute to the arsonist's flame.
And the youth were about their youthful business
of tranquillized vandalism, Temazepam sex,

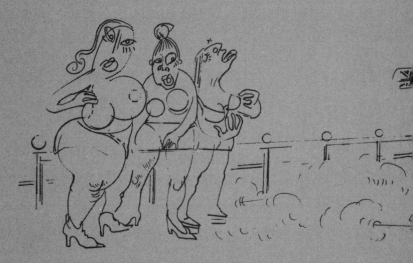

some on the brown going down on the ground,
drowning with joy in a fluidless vortex,
of casual car theft and chemical stargazing.
The youth, I would say, were just doing their job.
Some would call it low art, others plainly degrading.

For it was just another night at the seaside.
Just another shrill moped on the prom prom prom.
Just another chilled posse of corned-beef-legged girls
begging for action – and it all smelt so strong.

For it was just another night at the seaside.

51

The Large Child (He was never seven years old)

It was a very strange day when the large child
appeared in the playground.
Yes it was a very strange day indeed when that large child
appeared in the schoolyard.
He was an instant curiosity, for he had very hairy legs
for a seven year old.
He sang the school hymn in a very deep voice.
Oh yes it was a very strange day when that large child
smashed the school high-jump record set in 1973 by a similar
large child.

He was never seven years old,
seven and a half
seven and three-quarters maybe!
But never seven years old, oh no he wasn't, certainly not,
no way!

He wore the same uniform as all the other children
but it was too tight! It was far too tight, it was far too tight
indeed.
He formed a very unhealthy relationship

with the games teacher
Mrs Ruddock!
He was bigger, different with a very thick beard of hair on his
face.

He was never seven years old,
seven and a half
seven and three-quarters quite possibly.
But never seven years old, oh no he wasn't, certainly not,
no way!

After a while the children became used to the large child.
They forgave him for breaking the lavatory,
they forgave him for his peculiar body odour,
they forgave him for his bizarre behaviour in the
swimming pool,
they forgave him for being a large child.

But then, one day at the start of term approaching the
beginning of winter
when the leaves were falling from the trees

with a chill wind in the air and all the children
gathered together in small groups against the cold, waiting

for the final whistle to blow
another large child appeared
then another, then another
then another bigger still.
A group of *large* children!

Oh the headmistress let them stay, of course she did!
Because the school rugby team had become champions for the
first time since 1973 when a group of similar large children
had appeared, for no apparent reason.

She was missing the point.
She was drunk on success.
For while she sat in her office with her legs up on the table
pissing it up on sherry and smoking large Havanas with the
games teacher – Mrs Ruddock –
the large children ran rampant in the playground terrorizing all
who strayed in their giant paths.

Oh the lollipop ma – Mr Snitcher –
he tried to stop them, he tried to throw the book at them,
he tried to bring some sort of order to the proceedings.
But, oh he paid – *he paid!* A terrible, *terrible price!*

So it was a very strange day
when the large children singled aboard the small white
minibus
with the whole village watching.
Some people shook their fists in the air and shouted,

*'Go on, get out of it, you monsters. Sling yer hook
and never come back!'*

Others, spent a few moments alone to shed a quiet tear
but, if one person spoke for everyone
then it was Mr Snitcher the lollipop man
who shrieked from his wheelchair in a hysterical voice.

*'Seven years old – seven years old.
Not with having legs like that they weren't!*

*'Seven years old – seven years old
The child had a full beard of hair on his face.
Seven years old – seven years old
Somebody needs to have a word with somebody about
something because somebody's been having a laugh!'*

One Nation Under a Goatee

Give me now your goatee beard
Hand it over, give it here
Let me hold it in my hand
Chinny Goatee Beardy man

Give it up, give it in
Or put it in a beard-sized tin
And leave it by the barber's door
Because you know it is not yours!
Goatee man
Beardy man
Or do you have a bearded plan?
Will you travel around the world
With your furry friend unfurled?
Barefaced cheek but covered chin
Hand it over, hand it in
Hand it over, hand it in
Render unto me the hair
From your chinny chin chin.

The Leapin
Lagavu

The Leaping Haggis of Lagavulin

On a fair summer's eve west of the Firth of Forth
Where the heather runs thick and the sun sets late
Did three foolhardy Sassenachs meet with a rare,
                                    untimely fate.

For back in early eighty-nine
            when southern folks were feeling fine
When brokers from the working classes
            drank champagne from tall pint glasses
While the gents from Berks and Hants,
            in black Armani underpants,
Talked in drunken monotones
            about the price of mobile phones
Did three well-tailored gentlemen
            from deepest Kensington descend
Upon their local county inn
            and there my friends did they begin
To chart their own cruel destiny

For there they stood for all to see
Pontificating with such vigour
About their skill behind the trigger
Of their Purdey side-by-side shotguns
And how they'd skin the hide of anything
   be it man or beast
And hang it on their wall at least.

The bravado grew stronger
And the truth was stretched longer
Old family trees were produced with new branches
Country homes became piles
And piles became gout
And these men became giants with suitable stances
For hunched shoulders were dropped
Spinal cords were stretched long
Double chins became chiselled
And talk became song

As the old landlord smiled
And the hour grew late

'D'you know I am related to Henry the Eighth?'

Spoke Christopher Kennilworthe Bottlebank Smythe
Slashing the sabre he'd pulled from a beam side to side

'We were born far too late!'

Said one William Spanke-Harde
Bill Bodde said nothing
Just stared through his tankard's glass bottom
To watch the last customer leave
These latter-day lancers so fully deceived
That for all they said and all they claimed
       and all they stamped and all they flamed
They could not see where their three fine tales
       would rest
That the target they sought was nailed indeed
Upon their three fine foolish chests.
For as they stood propped up and preening
And the morning light approached
I could not say if they were dreaming
When a crackling laugh split the smoke
       and gas-filled air
Then a voice so deep so fine so rare

Smote the silence on their gin-filled banter
As they gaped at the falling tam-o'-shanter
Which flew through the air from the public bar
And landed astride one Bill Bodde's pint jar.

'Yae can drink a few pints
Yae can talk a good fight
But the last without the first
would be a rare canny sight
For do I hear the voices of gentlemen
For I hear their countless bullish claims
And ah've heard the stories of powder and shot
But ah'd like tae ken somethin'
ma brave boys just what
Would yae say if ah said there was a beast
That could'nae gie a tinker's curse
For all yer high-blown fancy talk
And all yer silk and double-cuff shirts
For he's never been caught an' he's never been seen
And but no-one's returned
from what must be umpteen
Expeditions to capture this strange wild creature

Abroad in the heather dear sirs ah beseech yae
You'll need more than Tanqueray

>   *and your old schoolin'*
> *To capture the Haggis of Lagavulin.'*

Now it must be said that Englishmen relish antagonists
And such a cunningly well-timed protagonist
Cut such a swathe through their brash undertakings
These sons of St George left the hostelry staking
Their honour and currency, keys to their cars
In a northward-bound taxi cab shouting 'Hussar!'

Oh they drove up the motorway and over the border
Checking their shotguns were oiled
>   and all in good order
Skirting west past of Glasgow
And on through Loch Lomond
Cast off on the Sound
And then they sailed low on the tide,
Oh the cool summer's mist
Did rise up to greet them
But could not calm the tempest
Which silently raged beneath clean green
>   Barbour jackets
And country suits bespoke by Hackett.

The ferryman winked and tipped them his cap
And asked them which day it would be
                they'd come back
He seemed sure they'd find what it was
                that they came for
And bid them good luck as they strode to the shore
But our heroes it will not surprise when I say
Held out-of-date tickets and only one way
And this is what they didn't hear the ferryman say:

'First he'll smell your fine smell
Then he'll ken why yae came
And it wil'nae be lang
'Fore he'll ken yae by name
Fa' he'll bend 'neath your windae
And sniff at your door
And it wil'nae be lang
'Fore he'll ken yae nae more
And your kinfolk will ask
                why you e'er went foolin'
Wi' the Loupin' Haggis of Lagavulin.

'Oh go back will yae boys

while yae still have the chance

Why no' go tae a place nice and quiet like France

Where you'll drink fizzy water

and eat runny cheese

And have food with your garlic

Dear sirs I would plead with yae

Please go back will yae

While you've the chance

Why no' go to a place nice and quiet like France.'

As their nostrils filled with the smoky reek
Of seaweed fused with burning peat
The memory of London's well-lit streets
Did fade with the day as the sea touched the sun
Oh the sky was turned crimson, the night had begun.

And what a night it was to prove.

Someone said someone heard
three shotgun shells cry out
Others disclaimed in their low whispered tone
That they'd heard the great beast
and its wild skirling shout
Three Barbour jackets were found on the ground
Three tattered suits near the foot of a mound

Three giant feathers found up on the black burn
And three shredded scalps blowing high on the cairn.

So for all they'd said and all they'd claimed
And all they'd stamped and all they'd flamed
For their old family trees and all their fine schooling
They could'nae catch the

Haggis of Lagavulin.

The Closet Heterosexual

Young Fred was gay the simple truth
For he was outed in his youth
He'd swing his bum from side to side
To court provincial diatribe
But quickly he moved up to town
Where people did no longer frown
At Fred's outlandish sense of dress
No, *au contraire*, they were impressed

'Ha-ha. Oh look, oh come see here,
There goes that funny little queer!'

Cried builders from the scaffold high
Or gentlemen in dark-brown ties
Who'd hiss and wink from limousines
Enquiring after Frederick's means
And ask him if he'd like employment
Blowing up balloons for fun
Or being filmed in fur pyjamas
Hunted down by men with guns

False, of course
And with no remorse
They sniffed their snuff
Yet lost its scent
And so to others paid their rent.

While Frederick's voice and charming smile
Brought men to travel many miles
To Auntie Phil's Espresso bar
They gave the cry of
'Ooh la la!'

When Frederick in his French beret
And Breton T-shirt there did play
Upon his best friend's naval squeezebox
A medley of hits from *Top of the Pops*
Oh how they'd howl in raptured glee

'Oh Frederick play this song for me!'

To tell the truth one must suppose
His fitted German lederhosen

May have added some attraction
To the gay Bavarian faction
Who stoutly stood with waxed moustaches
Making gruff Germanic passes
At a group of Belgian tailors
Carefully disguised as football players.

His popularity climbed and climbed
The hero of a modern kind
At clubs he'd walk straight past the queue
To *'Oohs!'* and *'Ahs!'* and *'How do you dos?'*
From proud and fawning club promoters
Feeling blessed by Frederick's smile
Their eyes would clock up dollar signs
For Fred was here they'd make a pile.

'Fred's here, Fred's here –
everybody's turning queer!'

The cry went up for miles around
From Clapham South to Kentish Town.

'Fred's here, Fred's here –
everybody's turning queer!'

The clergy came out in their droves
Even workmen digging roads
Judges from beneath their wigs
And even the police force.

Hurrah hurrah it was so gay
But then arrived the fateful day

When Frederick dressed in Westwood
    wicker G-string
Underneath his see-through shorts
His nipples tongue and armpits pierced
In chainmail sandals in he walked
With purple hair and feather boa
Skimpy T-shirt made from glass
On which the slogan clearly read:

'I'm gay and proud
        so kiss my arse!'

Frederick was led quickly through the ultraviolet bar
And put at the head of a table for ten
On a chair or more a throne with inscription 'FR'
And there he surveyed all the sycophants doffing
The priests and the judges quite nervously coughing
He smiled and raised them his Benylin bomb
And at that very moment the whole thing went
Terribly *terribly* wrong

      For something caught his sequinned eye
      Something made his mouth go dry
      Something made his blood run hot
      And friends that something should have not
      64-34-68

Enough to cause a minor earthquake
The ample bosom of Desdemona Shuttlecock
Made his pout part and his tongue drop
Into the rarefied nitrate-scented air
Then fast up his smooth cheek crept a lecherous glare
His nostrils flared open
His ears began smoking
White palms dripping wet with his naked desire
For this woman, this object
This piece of ripe rump
Was the one that watched Fred build his high funeral pyre

    Now I'd like to say he felt the heat
    That rose obscuring cold defeat
    That stared back at his brutal eye
    That someone gave a warning cry

'Oh Frederick no, oh not today,
    You'll give the wretched game away!
Oh don't! Oh no! You feckless fool!
    You're breaking all the blooming rules!'

But there was no supervision
Preventing imminent head-on collision.

His thoughts became whispers from quivering lips

    'My God, she's fucking asking for it!
    Look at those tits!
    Look at that arse!'

Whispers became murmurs, then shattering glass
Attracted all eyes as fate's hand dealt its blow
You are helpless my friends so relax for the show:

'*Get your tits out!*

Get your tits out!

Get your tits out!

For the lads!' He cried.

'*Get your tits out!*

Get your tits out!

Get your tits out!

For the lads!' He shrieked.

'*Get your tits out!*

Get your tits out!

Get your tits out!

For the lads-ah!'

The bar was empty.

Fred stood alone.

No more priests
No more judges
They'd scattered and flown
There was only one bus boy who remained, left behind
But with all due respect he was deaf, dumb and blind!

Now Frederick wears disguise in Soho
Especially down Old Compton Street
For when he's seen, there is a cry
That all the outraged folk repeat.

'Ha-ha. Oh look, oh come see here,
There goes that funny old ex-queer!
'Heterosexual! Heterosexual!
Lovely engine – where's your petrol?'

So be careful if you're outed
Heroes all and heroines
For how does the old proverb go?

'Far better to be outed
Than to be inned!'

The New Age Juggler

I should have never come to this place.
It was all such a reckless and ill-advised thought.
I should have seen the warning signs,
but like a sad fool I was stupidly caught on the hop.
I was sent to the shop,
to buy lamp oil or joss sticks.
Oh it was all such an obvious smokescreen,
but I fell for it,
turned my back,
he whipped his balls out in a flash.

The truth is I've lost my lover to a New Age juggler,
a man who throws hoops and balls in the air.
I've tried to learn three, but he can do seven,
there's no competition I'm lacking the flair.

He said to be cool and not spoil the vibe
because we are after all, Man, one –
                              and part of the same tribe.
(Oh those words came so easily from his lips)

With his beard painted blue and his Celtic tattoo
and his cheeky New Age juggler's smile.
With his mystical roots
and his paratroop boots
and his Trustafarian Gloucestershire pile.

Now I lay in the tent
so lonely and sad
whilst they laugh and giggle in my sleeping bag.
Well what would you do
if you were in my shoes?
Well I'll tell you exactly what I'm going to do!

I'm going to ransack his rucksack
pilfer his clubs,
half-inch his hoops,
then we'll see who's the mug!
I have seen his high rise
now I'll watch how he falls
I shall render him impotent –
a juggler with no balls!

The Tale of Edward Gallahad
(For half-baked parents)

Dear parents listen to my tale
For dutifully I must unveil
The story of an unfortunate lad
By the name of Edward Gallahad
An unpopular boy among his peers
But his parents loved him – that was only too clear
For they spoilt the child and spared the lash
In short they gave him too much cash
To tell the truth he found it funny
To chortle at the pocket money
Of boys with not as much as he
His chubby cheeks would flush with glee

'Ha-ha!' he'd cry. *'You're a frightful shower*
For I have greater spending power!'

And the power to spend indeed he had
For Edward was a hapless lad

He attended school but twice a week
For a woeful secret he began to keep
Yes Ed, he liked the baker's shop
And from dawn till dusk would stuff his chops
With chocolates, fancies and eclairs
And all the other sinful wares
That bakers' windows do display
For the eyes of little boys to prey.

Now on one particularly fateful morn
Between two large cakes dear Ed was torn
For one was chocolate double cream
And the other
ooh you should have seen
With strawberries, hazelnuts and so much more
It could have fed a family of four
But with a gluttonous smile Ed made his choice
To which the baker, in a trembling voice

Said, 'Sir, that is the eighth this week
This pace of eating you cannot keep
Please why not try a smaller cake
It will avoid a tummy ache.'

But Edward with a thunderous cry
Howled,

'Baker! That is a slanderous lie!'

He grabbed both cakes and hurried off
Towards the place where oft he'd scoff.

So down past the pig farm and over the footbridge
Our gluttonous friend walked his glutinous pilgrimage
But there by the roadside his beady young eye spied
A strange-looking chap in a faded red tracksuit

'Stand clear ragamuffin!' said Ed by now puffing

Flushed pink with exertion, *'Or you'll feel my boot!'*

The man looked up, thin, drawn with deep sunken eyes
Eyes a depth of green that gave surprise
Or even slightly paralysed this greedy little fellow
And on his back with two large straps
He had in place a cello
With hair thick like rope
And a look of such hope
First he stroked his long beard
And then rhythmically spoke.

'S'wa'appan lik'wboy?' the ragamuffin said.

'Please look 'pan I because me I 'ave no food dis day
So why na sheare dem cake dem wi' I an' I
An' 'pan dis cello me I go play a choown
Which gan'tekwey all dem keer
An' leave unu feeling peace righteous n'onelovein
In soul body mind 'tis true
'Tis even said to give new lease of life
To dem unhappy one who spend dem cash
On braad cream bwun.'

'How dare you speak to me like that!'
Bright red with fury Edward spat.

'And put that instrument away
For I wish not to hear it play
Or for that matter share my food
With such a smelly, dirty, crude unruly scruff
Who finds it funny to pester boys
With empty tummies!'

And with that Edward pushed aside
The hungry man whose bright-green eyes
Produced a sad forgiving look
And then in one long easy swoop
The cello from his back he took
And from his boot produced a bow

And played a note so sweet and low
That Edward's cares were sucked away
As further to the woods he strayed.

Now Ed was waddling through the woods
His arms piled high with pastry goods
Singing a song which more than likely
Was based on food when ever so lightly
Upon his shoulder he felt a tap
and turned to see one Myrtle Frogstrapp
A girl who was known for miles around
For a strange and elephantine sound
But no-one ever asked her why
She gave this strange, unworldly cry
For when the sound was heard abroad

Men, women and children cried, 'Oh Lord!
Quick hide away the pastry goods
For Myrtle's coming from the woods!'

*'Phueeeeeeewrpph,'** cried Myrtle. *'Give me cake.'*

And Edward in his boots did quake
But like a cowardly little fellow
He turned and ran so Myrtle bellowed,

'Phueeeeeeewrpph.'

Edward stopped clean cold in his tracks
A shiver ran screaming down his back

*To represent the sound of an elephant.

He turned to say please take the cakes
But by this time it was too late.
To tell you friends what happened that night
I do confess would not be right
But let me tell you Edward paid
In full for all his wicked ways
Now that's the peril dear congregation
Of self-indulgent, misdirected, juvenile mastication
Childhood wallets stuffed with moolah
Will end in nought but a frightful hooha
So perchance you hear a haunting bellow
Think of Ed that poor young fellow
Think first to the depths to which his poor dear life
had sunk.

And think last of the suction power...of an elephant's trunk!

Phueeeeeeewrpph!

The Ill-Mar

The Ill-Mannered Alien

A spacecraft landed in my garden
A creature came out and knocked at my door
It took under twenty-five seconds
To see we just didn't get on at all.

It was ignorant and rude
It was arrogant and crude
And it didn't wipe its tentacles on entering my home
It belched and it farted till the moment it departed
I'm not surprised the dreadful beast was travelling alone.

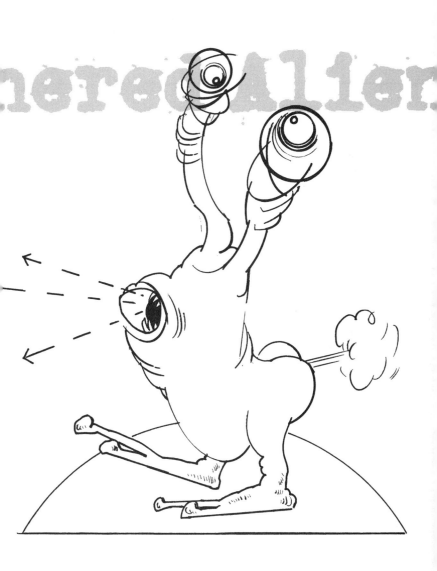

The Tale of Molly

Now that I have your rapt attention
I feel it my duty to sorrowfully mention
A tale of thoughtless youthful folly
Concerning a girl whose name is Molly.

Now Molly the child was sadly christened
For as the congregation listened
To the curate's pious benediction
The poor dear child was struck with an affliction
That would haunt her life like a mistimed…joke
Yes it all began with holy smoke
For as the thurible the thurifer swung
A heavy cloud of incense hung
And snaked its wily winding way
To where the chubby infant lay.

Now those of you with weakened hearts
Please shield your ears before I start
To exhume the corpse of a tale so dark
That it's never gone beyond Finsbury Park

of Molly

And many of the locals there
Still walk around with upright hair.

But back to the service and back to the church
Young Molly with a frenzied lurch
Sat up and sucked the scented plume
Then rolled her eyes around the room
She gave a frightful scream that shook the air
A scream that made the curate glare
A mad shrill cry that made the stained-glass windows smash
And yes, dear friends, I think you've guessed

The child was sadly mashed, or stoned, or high,
or out of her tree

For as much as she gurgled no-one could see
That the bairn approached a state of Zen
Except for wicked Uncle Len
Whose curly hair hung down below his yellow denim flares
For Uncle Leonard lived a life of festivals and fairs
He often attended pagan rites

And danced with druids in the night
Yes, Uncle Len could sense the vibe
For he was once one of Spiral Tribe
A bunch of vagabonds and rogues
Who tore around the country roads
Making camp in woodland glade
And holding parties they used to call raves
Where youngsters sang and danced all night
As if they'd swallowed dynamite.
But Leonard knew by now
That he could not say what he'd seen
For who'd believe a New Age traveller hippy
That they had all seen
On television just last Wednesday
Talking of the Mother Earth
Telling tales of magic mushrooms – spiritual rebirth.

How embarrassing...

So blissful in innocence
Aunt Millicent whistled and snored
Whilst Leonard shrugged his Afghan coat
And walked away towards the door.

But let us take a leap in time
Young Molly grew up strong and fine
To Switzerland she went to school
Oh how she made those Swiss boys drool
Well-schooled and bred her social set
Comprised of diplomats and debs

Society journals said that she
Was romantically linked with royalty
Then one night at a glittering gala ball
Young Molly at first was quite appalled
When best friend Bunny Farquharson

Said, *'To the powder room you must come*
For Crown Prince Al Bebe of South Brunaid
Is holding court with a razor blade.
Oh do come Molly, do let's try
I wish so much to get so high!'

Chop chop chop went the Prince's blade
As the fine white lines 'cross the table were laid

'Darling Bebe!' snorted Bunny

'This is Molly – she's my chum.'

'Molly you're so beautiful
I'm very nearly overcome,'

Said Al Bebe directing the girl to indulge
His eye displaying a right royal bulge
Half from narcotics and half from his lust
As he settled his eyes on the heaving bust
Of the girl he'd decided to take for his mate
So with pupils beginning to gently dilate
Dear Molly was swept from her silk-finished heels
As she fingered the keys to his glittering wheels.

Now one hour later wide and bright
Dear Molly's eyes did show her plight
Driving in the Prince's car
An XJ220 Jaguar
But oh dear friend when on cocaine
The world does not seem quite the same
And Prince Al Bebe paid the cost
For thinking he was Alain Prost

Crash! Bang! Tinkle! Wallop! Splat!

The Jaguar was squashed quite flat
The super car was concertinaed
And so my friends I think that we had better
Cut out from the wreckage
Morality or some high message
Involving opinion or topical point
Or maybe just light up another great joint
Or join up with Bunny quite out of her head
And, why not, for tomorrow
We may all be dead!

Dub Band

It was a kind of Afro-Celtic
Folk-goth-dub thing.

She played a nine-string bass violin
Which went through a cry-baby wah-wah fuzz tone.

And he played a pair of fossilized mammoth bones.

Their bodies were naked
smeared with red and blue paint.
The desert sage that hung in the air
caused many people to stagger and faint.

A spiritual tremble ran down my spine
and then without warning
I just started to cry.

It was primal and edgy.
It was tribal and chic.
And all with an ambient disco beat.

You really should have been there.

MTV Party

Simply everyone's going to the MTV party
And everyone's getting there an hour after it started
Because everybody's sophisticated and everybody's cool
And everybody knows the score
And knows just what to do.

MWAH ✳ MWAH ✳ *darling*
                              I haven't seen you since Cannes
Let me introduce myself for I must be my biggest fan

So fax me on my mobile, call me when you can
I've got a window about four-thirty
Unless, of course, I make other plans
So, do let's do lunch darling
We'll talk it all over, we'll go frame by frame
So I'll see you later alligator

Ciao Ciao, tiger!

What was her name?

Liberty

It isn't safe to walk the streets,
so I shall beat a fast retreat.
    There are too many people on the Planet Earth,
    there are too many mothers giving too much birth.
There's a hole in the ozone layer,
someone told me God was a basketball player.
    There's pollution in the sea,
    needles in the sand.
So I have elected to wear fake tan
    and hang in the air-conditioned world
    of Ben 'n' Jerry and teenage girls.
Like a baby in a womb
or a corpse in a tomb
    I couldn't give a damn because I can't stand the fumes.
    Give me liberty or give me plastic surgery

I am *not* coming out from the shopping mall!

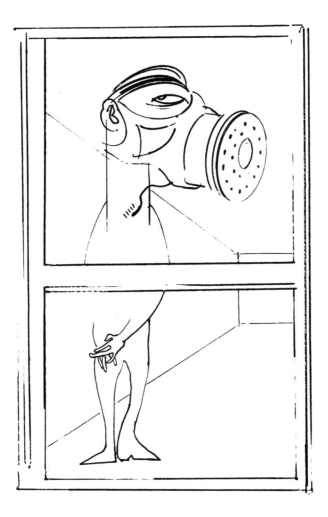

The Cyber Tragedy*

I don't go out I just stay in and I go to the cyber café.
I meet all my friends and have such a good time
when I go to the cyber café.
Last year I went to a cyber disco
it was really a lot of fun.
I danced the whole night with a wonderful girl
who looked just like Pamela Anderson. Well, virtually.

Yeah we fell for each other and got virtually drunk,
then had virtual sex in the back of her car.
She e-mailed and said she was virtually pregnant
and never intended to go quite so far.
What could I do? I virtually loved her
I did the virtually decent thing.
We were wed in a cyber chapel of love
I gave her my virtual diamond ring.

*To be spoken in a German accent.

Tragedy

I felt so happy I virtually cried
I told all my friends at the cyber café
I wed the most wonderful virtual girl on this virtually
wonderful day.

But news came back and I was virtually sick
for my bride I was told by my virtual best friend
was known as a virtual serial bigamist
married to three thousand other men.

I nearly virtually killed myself.
I nearly virtually strung myself up.
I came close to joining a cyber monastery
becoming a virtual monk.

But then it got worse.
It got much, much worse.
For a terrible thing had gone undetected
we'd taken no proper precautions

I'd left my modem unprotected!

I was struck down by a virtual virus.
It scrambled my data and wiped my disk.
I felt such a virtual idiot,
but I'd no real excuse for I'd known all the risks.

Now I just weep by my keyboard
surrounded in despondency shrouded in gloom.
But, as Mother says:

> *'Things can't be ... really ... so bad.'*

Because if I don't want to
I never really need come out of my bedroom.

Skye

See the curve of the Earth

See the snow-covered hills

See the mountain, the sea

See your own clouded view

See your home and your friends

See the rocks on the shore

See your troubles

Your birth

Your God

Your life

Your death

For one moment be still

Think of nothing.

The Soul of a Drowning Man

You are such a beautiful monster

You are full of fanciful flowing delight

You know you have stolen my heart

with your whisper

Sweet sister I will be your lover tonight

Let me lie in your arms my own sweetheart

Kiss my forehead and pull me away from the shore

Take me deep in your love

To a place I can be

Far away from the fray

Let me breathe again

Hardcore Techno Unplugged

Hardcore techno unplugged.

The DJ put the needle
in the groove

Nothing happened at all.

Hardcore techno unplugged.

It was really really quiet
but really really really cool

Hardcore techno unplugged.

Then everyone started
dancing but all at
different speeds

It was the start of something

amazing

At least I heard it was.

Till Death Do Us Part

They met in a hut on the outskirts of town
They dressed in black, they made no sound
They came on foot and some on bike
They came in the deepest dead of night
They came to pledge their mortal soul

To heavy metal rock 'n' roll

First they gathered in a ring
Then began to chant and sing

We love speed core
We love thrash
We love the hammer and the anvil crash
Metal is deep within my heart so

until death do us part

Then they all played air guitars
And moshed till dawn 'neath the summer stars

And wondered will I *ever* meet a *real* girl?

Green

Green Ocean

My bath lies like a smouldering green ocean
Molten heart and still desire
Expectant seductive invitingly patient
But far too hot to jump in just yet

Bathtime oh the great continuum
Watcher on my mortal journey
Silent shrine to contemplation
Far too warm to jump out just yet

The Solo Project

Well,
It's dark and moody, very distinctive
Simple in texture with an anthmic tinge
Symphonically progressive, thoroughly impressive
Alternative mainstream with a synth rock twinge.

It's kinda Beck meets Bush meets Geggy Tah
Sorta Pulp meets Hole meets Verve meets Gwar.
Think of ethereal Christian surf goth blended with
psychedelic lesbian swamp rock.

Half pop half punk half death core
It's kinda Vegas Brit pop, but much much more.
Much much more.

Yeah, it's a solo project.

The Storm

Storm froze the horse's head

Pine cracked and earth bled

Pounding waves and screaming wind

Saltern rain and mist descend

Boulders thunder on the spray

Shrouded skies of mantle grey

Plunging down in wingless flight

To meet an ocean's appetite

The Lover's Flight

Speak to me not sweet wounded woman
 Tell me not now of whom I might be
Unfasten me from your bleeding bow
 Release me from your burning wheel
For I shall take sleep, oh beauty
 I shall take dreams over earthward-bound cares
I shall fly high over mortal man's head
 Twist freely between his rising prayer

Speak to me not then my angel
 I know I will love you upon my deep dreams
Let other men pull at your fragile heart
 I'll see you glow bright no trace of a seam
So go freely sweet spirit go swiftly
 Leave now whilst you can lest the wind does change
And let me not touch your tender lips
 Lest I should never dream again.